Freddy Adu

José María Obregón

English translation: Megan Benson

PowerKiDS press™

Editorial Buenas Letras™

New York

Published in 2009 by The Rosen Publishing Group, Inc.
29 East 21st Street, New York, NY 10010

First Edition

Editor: Nicole Pristash
Book Design: Nelson Sa
Layout Design: Julio Gil

Photo Credits: Cover (left), p. 21 © MLS/Getty Images; cover (right), pp. 5, 7, 9, 11, 13, 15, 19 © Getty Images; p. 17 © AFP/Getty Images.

Library of Congress Cataloging-in-Publication Data

Obregón, José María, 1963–
   Freddy Adu / José María Obregón. — 1st ed.
      p. cm. — (World soccer stars = Estrellas del fútbol mundial)
   English and Spanish.
   Includes bibliographical references and index.
   ISBN 978-1-4358-2730-1 (library binding)
   1. Adu, Freddy, 1989– —Juvenile literature. 2. Soccer players—United States—
Biography—Juvenile literature. I. Title.
   GV942.7.A34O37 2009
   796.334092—dc22
   [B]
                                            2008028324

Manufactured in the United States of America

Contents

1 Meet Freddy Adu 4

2 The Young Star 10

3 Playing in Europe 16

Glossary 22

Resources 23

Index 24

Contenido

1 Conoce a Freddy Adu 4

2 Una joven estrella 10

3 Rumbo a Europa 16

Glosario 22

Recursos 23

Índice 24

Freddy Adu is a soccer player. Adu was born on June 2, 1989. His full name is Fredua Koranteng Adu.

Freddy Adu es jugador de fútbol. Adu nació el 2 de junio de 1989. Su nombre completo es Fredua Koranteng Adu.

4

Adu was born in the city of Tema, in Ghana. Ghana is an African country. Adu's family moved to the United States when he was eight years old.

Adu nació en la ciudad de Tema, en Ghana. Ghana es un país de África. Cuando Adu tenía 8 años, su familia se mudó a los Estados Unidos.

When Adu was young, he played soccer with children much older than him. He became very good at the game.

Cuando Adu era pequeño jugaba con chicos más grandes que él. Así, Adu se convirtió en un mejor jugador de fútbol.

In 2004, Adu became a member of the team D.C. United. He was the youngest player in Major League Soccer, or MLS. MLS is the United States' soccer league. Adu was 14 years old!

En 2004, Adu se unió al equipo D.C. United en la MLS. Adu se convirtió en el jugador más joven de la MLS. La MLS es la liga de fútbol de los Estados Unidos. ¡Adu tenía 14 años!

Adu plays midfielder and forward positions. As a midfielder, Adu passes the ball to other players. As a forward, he scores **goals**.

Adu juega en la posición de medio volante y la de delantero. Como medio volante se encarga de pasar la pelota a otros jugadores. Como delantero, Adu **anota** goles.

In 2007, Adu was the U.S. team captain in the U-20 **World Cup** in Canada. This is the World Cup for players under the age of 20.

En 2007, Adu fue el capitán de la selección de los Estados Unidos en el Mundial sub-20, en Canadá. Esta es la **Copa del Mundo** para jugadores menores de 20 años.

In 2007, Adu also became a member of the Benfica soccer club, in Portugal. Benfica is one of the best clubs in Europe. In 2008, he **joined** the team Monaco, in France.

En 2007, Adu se unió al equipo Benfica de Portugal. El Benfica es uno de los mejores equipos de fútbol de Europa. En 2008, Adu se **unió** al Mónaco de Francia.

In 2008, Adu helped the U.S. team **qualify** for the 2008 Beijing **Olympics**. He had always wanted to play in the Olympic Games.

En 2008, Adu ayudó al equipo olímpico de los Estados Unidos a **clasificar** para las **Olimpíadas** de Pekín 2008. Adu siempre quiso participar en los juegos olímpicos.

Adu has a lot of fans around the world. Adu often shakes hands with them after his games.

Adu tiene muchos admiradores alrededor del mundo. Con frecuencia Adu saluda a sus seguidores al acabar el partido.

Glossary / Glosario

goals (gohlz) When people put the ball in the net to score points.

joined (joynd) Took part in.

Olympics (oh-lim-piks) Games held every four years for athletes all over the world.

qualify (kwah-lih-fy) To meet the requirements of something.

World Cup (wur-uld kup) A group of soccer games that takes place every four years with teams from around the world.

---

anotar Conseguir uno o varios goles.

clasificar Quedar seleccionado en una competición deportiva.

Copa del Mundo (la) Competición de fútbol, cada 4 años, en la que juegan los mejores equipos del mundo.

Olimpíadas (las) Competición deportiva mundial que se realiza cada cuatro años.

unirse Formar parte de un grupo o equipo.

Resources / Recursos

Books in English/Libros en inglés

Shea, Therese. *Soccer Stars*. Danbury, CT:
Children's Press, 2007.

Bilingual Books/Libros bilingües

Obregón, José María. *David Beckham*. New York:
Rosen Publishing/Buenas Letras, 2008.

Web Sites

Due to the changing nature of Internet links,
Rosen Publishing has developed an online list of
Web sites related to the subject of this book. This
site is updated regularly. Please use this link to
access the list:

www.buenasletraslinks.com/ss/freddy/

Index

A
Africa, 6

B
Benfica, 16

G
Ghana, 6

M
Major League
    Soccer (MLS), 10

O
Olympics, 18

U
United States, 6

W
World Cup, 14

Índice

A
África, 6

B
Benfica, 16

C
Copa del Mundo, 14

E
Estados Unidos, 6

G
Ghana, 6

M
MLS, 10

O
Olimpíadas, 18

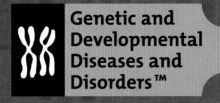

Genetic and Developmental Diseases and Disorders ™

Spina Bifida

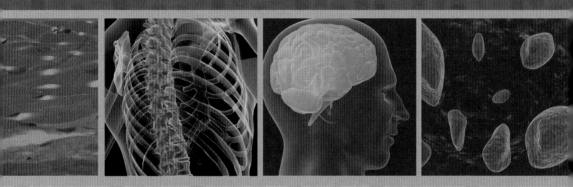

Stephanie Watson

New York

Published in 2009 by The Rosen Publishing Group, Inc.
29 East 21st Street, New York, NY 10010
www.rosenpublishing.com

Library of Congress Cataloging-in-Publication Data

Watson, Stephanie, 1969–
Spina bifida / Stephanie Watson. — 1st ed.
    p.cm.—(Genetic and developmental diseases and disorders)
Includes bibliographical references and index.
ISBN-13: 978-1-4042-1853-6 (library binding)
1. Spina bifida. I. Title.
RJ496.S74W38 2008
618.92'73—dc22

                                            2007040004

Manufactured in Malaysia

On the cover: Background: A scanning electron micrograph shows two
nerve cells *(red)* in the gray matter of the spinal cord that are surrounded
by nerve tissue. Foreground: A photograph of the spinal cord.

Contents

Introduction 4

1 Spina Bifida: Past and Present 9

2 A Genetics Primer 16

3 Who Gets Spina Bifida and What Can
Be Done to Treat It? 24

4 The Search for a Cure 37

5 The Future of Spina Bifida Research 46

Timeline 50

Glossary 53

For More Information 55

For Further Reading 58

Bibliography 59

Index 61

Introduction

The spinal cord is the road by which messages travel from the brain to the body and back. It is made up of many nerves. Any damage to this pathway can stop the flow of information. Without messages from the brain, the body can be left unable to walk, use the bathroom, and perform other important functions.

Sometimes, the spinal cord can be injured in childhood or adulthood, such as in an accident. But in other cases, it can be damaged very early in life, while the fetus is still growing in its mother's womb. In the fetus, the spinal cord grows out of a tiny piece of tissue called the neural tube. The top of this tube will form the baby's brain, and the rest of the tube will make up the spinal cord. The neural tube finishes forming and closes at the end of the first month of pregnancy.

In about one out of every one thousand babies, the neural tube doesn't close properly. This failure to close causes a defect in the spinal cord and in the small bones of the spine (vertebrae). This defect is called spina bifida.

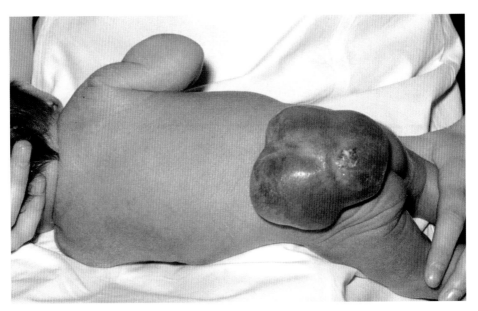

Babies born with the most severe form of spina bifida, called myelomeningocele, have an opening in the back. A sac containing the protective coatings of the spine and spinal nerves sticks out of this hole.

Spina bifida is the most common of a group of birth defects called neural tube defects. Anencephaly is the other common, and most severe, neural tube defect, in which the top end of the neural tube doesn't close and part of the brain and skull are missing. Babies born with anencephaly are usually blind, deaf, and not awake (unconscious). Many do not live long past birth. Another type of neural tube defect is encephalocele, in which the brain and coverings of the brain and spinal cord (meninges) stick out from the back of a baby's head. Surgery can fix this problem shortly after birth, but babies can have vision problems or even blindness if the defect is severe.

The outlook for people with spina bifida is far better. In fact, more than seventy thousand people today live with spina bifida, according to the Spina Bifida Association. With early recognition, prompt treatment, and regular therapy, people with this condition can live very fulfilling lives.

Types of Spina Bifida

When people say "spina bifida," they're usually talking about the most severe form of the disease, called myelomeningocele (or sometimes meningomyelocoele). Two other forms of the disease exist, and one is so mild that people are sometimes not even aware they have it.

The three types of spina bifida are the following:

Spina bifida occulta. This form is often called hidden spina bifida because it is so mild that it frequently doesn't cause any obvious symptoms. In fact, the only way some people find out they have it is when they have an X-ray for some other reason. About 10 to 20 percent of otherwise healthy people have spina bifida occulta, according to the Spina Bifida Association.

With this condition, there is a small opening in the vertebrae of the spinal column but no damage to the spinal cord itself. The only outward sign of spina bifida occulta is a small patch of hair, dimple, darker-colored skin, or swelling in the skin over the affected vertebrae. These markings are seen on the lower back, usually over the sacrum, which is the flat set of bones just above the buttocks. Because the spinal cord itself isn't damaged, spina bifida occulta usually doesn't need any treatment.

Meningocele. This is the rarest type of spina bifida. In this form, the spine is open and a sac (called the meningocele) pokes out through the hole. The sac contains the coatings (meninges) that protect the spinal cord and some spinal fluid, but the spinal cord itself is not affected. The sac can be removed with surgery. Most people with this condition have only mild disabilities.

Myelomeningocele. The name for this very serious condition comes from the Greek words *myelo* for "spine" and *cele* for "swelling." It's also known as open spina bifida.

Babies born with myelomeningocele have an opening in the back, from which both the protective coatings of the spine and the nerves of the spinal cord jut out. Sometimes, skin covers the sac. In other cases, the spinal cord is exposed, leaving the baby at risk for dangerous infections. Many years ago, babies who had myelomeningocele would die from infection shortly after birth. Today, most babies survive after having surgery to close their backs shortly after birth.

Because it affects the nerves of the spinal cord, myelomeningocele can leave the legs paralyzed. The higher up on the back the damage occurs, the more severely the person is paralyzed. Myelomeningocele can also make it hard for children to urinate and have a bowel movement because they are unable to work the muscles that control these functions. It can also be difficult for these children to sense when they have to go to the bathroom due to the nerve damage.

Most babies with this condition will have another complication called hydrocephalus, which is a collection of too much cerebrospinal fluid (CSF). Hydrocephalus is also known as "water on the brain." This condition occurs when the spinal defect prevents the fluid that protects the brain and spinal cord from draining normally. Fluid builds up around the brain, causing pressure to rise inside the head. This can lead to seizures, problems with the nervous system, or mental retardation if it isn't treated right away.

Why Do People Get Spina Bifida?

Scientists aren't sure exactly why people get spina bifida. They believe it has to do with a combination of genes and the environment. A person might have certain genes that put him or her at risk for spina bifida, then something in the environment triggers the disease.

A major environmental trigger for spina bifida is a lack of folic acid in the mother's diet during pregnancy. One of the best ways to prevent spina bifida is to take folic acid vitamins for a few months before getting pregnant and during the pregnancy. Folic acid is a B vitamin that is important for the body to function properly and for the fetus to grow. It is found in foods such as broccoli, spinach, and orange juice. Today, companies routinely add folic acid to pasta, cereal, and bread products. Folic acid is especially important during the first three months (or first trimester) of pregnancy, when the neural tube is forming and closing.

Folic acid has a clear connection to spina bifida, but pinning down the genetic causes of spina bifida hasn't been as easy. Researchers have found a few genes that they believe increase the risk, and they are on the hunt for more genes. They hope that finding spina bifida genes will one day lead to better treatments—or even a cure for this disease.

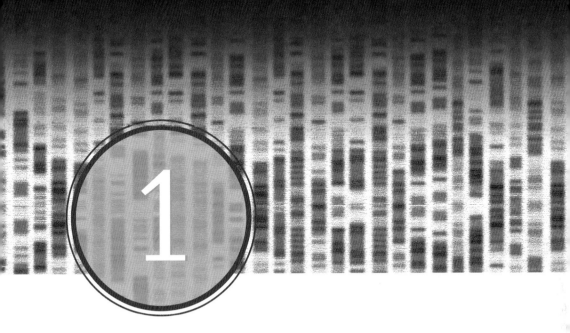

Spina Bifida: Past and Present

Scientists study clues from the past to help them track the history of certain diseases. From the evidence they have found, they believe that spina bifida has existed for thousands of years.

Skeletons discovered in a cave in Taforalt, Morocco, showed signs of spina bifida. The bones date back to between 10000 and 8500 BCE. Because of the large numbers of abnormal skeletons there, researchers believe that spina bifida was common among people who lived in this part of Morocco. Many skeletons in Peru that date back to about 5000 BCE also had abnormal spines that could have been caused by spina bifida.

Scientists have found evidence of the disease in the skeletons of ancient Egyptians. Archaeologists dug up 272 skeletons in the city of Giza that they believe date back to the time in which the pyramids were built (around the twenty-fifth century BCE). About 3 percent of the skeletons showed signs of spina bifida occulta.

The ancient Greek philosopher Aristotle (384–322 BCE) and the physician Hippocrates (c. 460–370 BCE) both supposedly knew about spina bifida and its complication, hydrocephalus. However, the disease wasn't reported in very early medical books because babies with spina bifida died so soon after birth that doctors weren't able to study them.

 ## Describing Spina Bifida

The first real explanation of spina bifida didn't come until the mid-1600s, when Dutch anatomist Nicolaas Tulp (1593–1674) named the disease and described its effects on the children who had it. (Tulp is probably best known as the demonstrator pictured in Dutch artist Rembrandt's 1632 masterpiece entitled *Anatomy Lesson*). In his 1641 book, *Observationes Medicae*, Tulp shared what he had learned from observing several patients with the disease.

The next big discovery came from Giovanni Battista Morgagni (1682–1771), the Italian doctor who is considered the father of modern pathology (the study of disease). In 1761, Morgagni described hydrocephalus, and he connected it to spina bifida.

In 1875, the German doctor Rudolf Virchow (1821–1902) came up with the name "spina bifida occulta" for the mildest form of the disease. Another German doctor, Hans Chiari (1851–1916), described in 1891 the abnormal structures in the brains of some children with spina bifida in which the lower part of the brain (cerebellum) stuck out into the upper part of the spinal column. These abnormalities were named

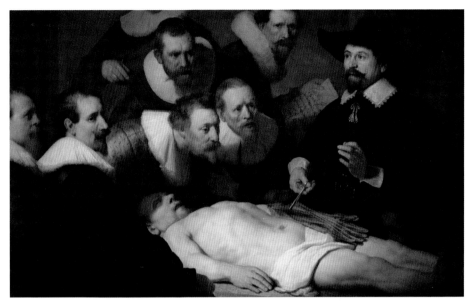

Dr. Nicolaas Tulp (the man who named spina bifida) is depicted standing over a body he is about to dissect in *The Anatomy Lesson* (1632), a masterpiece painted by the Dutch artist Rembrandt.

Chiari type II malformations (also called Arnold-Chiari malformations), and they can cause problems of the nervous system if not found and corrected. A less severe form of this brain abnormality is called the Chiari type I malformation, which does not usually occur with spina bifida. This malformation often does not cause symptoms and is usually found by chance when a person has an X-ray for other problems.

Early Treatments

At first, the only way to treat spina bifida was to remove the sac on the baby's spine or to drain the liquid from inside it. This

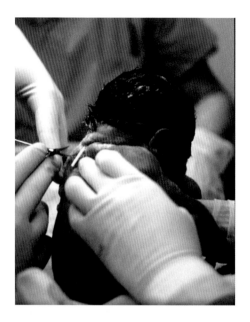

This newborn baby had a shunt implanted in his brain to correct hydrocephalus two months previously, while he was still in his mother's womb.

surgery was rarely successful—most patients died of infection. By the 1800s, doctors had found safer ways of removing the sac, but infection of the skin over it and the spinal fluid inside was still a problem.

In the early twentieth century, new techniques let doctors close the opening without causing a deadly infection. However, the children who had surgery were almost always left seriously disabled.

A major advancement in the treatment of spina bifida came in 1952 with the introduction of the shunt. The shunt was used to drain fluid and reduce pressure in the brain caused by hydrocephalus. By the 1960s, doctors had started to operate on babies with spina bifida soon after birth, and death rates from the disease began to drop.

By the 1990s, the survival rate among children with spina bifida had risen to 90 percent. Late in that decade, there was a major breakthrough. Some doctors were able to do surgery before babies with spina bifida were even born. While the

THE JOHN LORBER CONTROVERSY

In 1971, an English doctor named John Lorber (1915–1996) published a study of 524 patients who were born with spina bifida. He noted that about half of the infants died, even after they were treated with surgery. Most of the babies who did survive had serious physical problems.

Based on his research, Lorber came up with certain factors to help doctors decide how to treat their patients with spina bifida. Lorber based the factors on the quality of life he thought the babies might have. Based on these factors, he decided which babies should have surgery to close their spines shortly after birth and which ones would most likely die and thus should not receive treatment. Lorber thought surgery wouldn't be worthwhile or would be too painful for babies with the most severe effects of spina bifida, such as hydrocephalus and total paralysis.

Doctors began using Lorber's method to categorize spina bifida patients and their need for surgery, but the death rate of children with spina bifida grew much higher. Today, doctors are better able to treat spina bifida, and Lorber's techniques are no longer used.

mother was still pregnant, they could carefully operate on the fetus and close its back with a skin patch. Researchers are now trying to find out whether doing the surgery before the baby is born is better than doing surgery after birth to prevent the paralysis, hydrocephalus, and need for shunting that can occur in children with spina bifida. A large study to answer this question is currently under way at several major national medical centers.

Taking folic acid before getting pregnant and in the first few months of pregnancy can cut a baby's risk of getting spina bifida by more than half.

Modern Discoveries

In 1965, doctors Richard Smithells and E. D. Hibbard made a very important announcement in the *Lancet* medical journal. They had made the connection between folic acid and neural tube defects. They noted that taking folic acid before getting pregnant and during pregnancy could help prevent these diseases.

The finding was big news. Not all women got the message, though. Many still did not take extra folic acid before and during their pregnancies. So, organizations such as the March of Dimes began getting the word out about folic acid. In 1998, the U.S. government began requiring companies that make bread, pasta, and other grain products to fortify their foods with folic acid. Since then, the number of babies born with spina bifida has gone down.

In the early 1970s, researchers found a way to test babies for spina bifida before birth. Doctors D. J. Brock and R. G. Sutcliffe

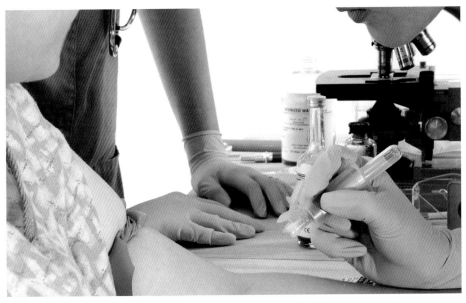

Nurses prepare a female patient for drawing a sample of her blood. Physicians can perform tests for spina bifida and other neural tube defects on a pregnant patient's blood sample by using the maternal alpha-fetoprotein test and the triple screen and quad screen tests.

of Edinburgh, Scotland, first discovered that high levels of a substance called alpha-fetoprotein in the fluid around the fetus (amniotic fluid) meant that a baby was likely to be born with neural tube defects. A year later, doctors also found a link between these diseases and high alpha-fetoprotein levels in the mother's blood.

These findings led to a new test for spina bifida and other neural tube defects called the maternal alpha-fetoprotein test. In this test, the doctor takes a sample of a pregnant woman's blood and tests the levels of alpha-fetoprotein. Newer versions of this test, called the triple screen and quad screen tests, also check for other substances that are affected by neural tube defects and other developmental problems.

A Genetics Primer

2

Your body is made up of *trillions* of cells. Inside each of those cells are the instructions to make you who you are. Those instructions are housed in the cell nucleus in structures called chromosomes.

Chromosomes are made up of strands of genetic material called deoxyribonucleic acid, or DNA. A piece of DNA looks like a twisted ladder. Scientists call this ladder a double helix. The sides of the ladder are made up of a sugar-phosphate combination, and the rungs are made from pairs of nitrogen bases: adenine (A) pairs with thymine (T), and cytosine (C) pairs with guanine (G). These pairs are connected by hydrogen bonds.

Sections of these letter sequences are called genes. Each gene or group of genes contains

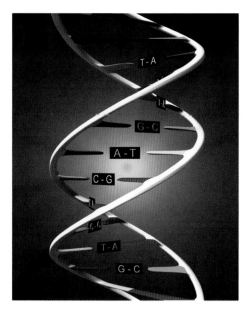

A DNA molecule has a double helix structure and looks like a twisted ladder. The sides of the ladder are made up of sugar and phosphate, and the rungs are pairs of nitrogen bases. Sections of DNA contain the genetic code for making proteins.

the code for producing a specific protein. Those proteins control every single one of the functions in your body, from your heartbeat to your hair color.

Most of the cells in the body contain forty-six chromosomes. The exceptions are sperm and egg cells, which each contain twenty-three chromosomes. When they meet to form an embryo, the chromosomes in the sperm and egg combine. The baby inherits half of its genes from his or her mother and the other half from his or her father. That is how traits are passed down from generation to generation, and it's why you might have been told that you have your "mother's eyes" or your "father's smile."

Pioneering Genetic Researchers

To most people, the pea plant isn't the most exciting member of the natural world. But to Austrian monk Gregor Mendel (1822–1884), pea plants were absolutely fascinating. Mendel

MUTANT GENES

Usually, the process of making a human being goes pretty smoothly. Sometimes, though, a problem can occur in the genetic code. Bases can be missing, added, or in the wrong place in the sequence. Without the right code, the protein isn't produced correctly, and the cells don't perform the right functions.

Diseases can result from these changes, or mutations. In some cases, the change is small enough that it is invisible or causes only minor problems. For example, a genetic mutation might give somebody a slightly unusually curved ear. In other cases, the mutation affects an important set of instructions, thereby leading to a serious disease. Examples of genetic diseases are Down syndrome (a condition that affects mental and physical development) and Huntington's disease (a disease that destroys nerve cells in the brain).

Parents can pass these genetic mutations and the diseases they cause to their children. Today, scientists are working hard to discover the reasons for genetic mutations. They hope that one day they will be able to fix these mutations before they can cause disease.

was interested less in the plants themselves than in an important clue they provided. By crossing different types of pea plants, Mendel discovered how traits, such as color, passed from one plant generation to another.

A contemporary of Mendel's, Charles Darwin (1809–1882), proposed another interesting idea about how traits pass through

In his book *The Origin of Species*, British scientist Charles Darwin proposed that animals adapt to their environment and pass those adapted traits down to their offspring in a process called natural selection.

generations. In 1859, he published a book called *The Origin of Species*. In it, Darwin suggested that all living things adapt in order to survive. For example, the giraffe's long neck evolved over time to help it reach the leaves in tall trees. Darwin said that when new traits help a species survive, animals can pass those traits on to future generations. He called this process natural selection.

How exactly the inherited traits that Mendel and Darwin described passed from parents to their children was still a mystery, though. Then in 1869, a Swiss biochemist named Johann Friedrich Miescher (1844–1895) discovered a new substance in the white blood cells he saw in a sample of pus. He named the substance "nuclein" because he found it in the cell nucleus. Today, scientists call this substance DNA, and they now know that it is what carries traits from parents to their offspring.

Myths and Facts

Myth: People with spina bifida are not as smart as those who don't have the disease.
Fact: Spina bifida usually does not affect mental function, so people with the condition often do just as well in school as their friends.

Myth: Most children who have spina bifida have to use a wheelchair.
Fact: Many people with spina bifida have the mildest form of the disease and don't have any trouble walking. Even those with the most severe kind of spina bifida can often walk with the help of braces.

Myth: If spina bifida doesn't run in her family, a woman doesn't need to take folic acid while she's pregnant.
Fact: Even babies without a family history of spina bifida can get the disease. Folic acid may reduce the risk of spina bifida by up to 70 percent. Every woman needs to take folic acid before she gets pregnant and during her pregnancy.

Into the Twentieth Century

Progress in genetic research sped forward in the 1900s. One of the major breakthrough moments came in the spring of 1953, when American scientist James Watson (1928–) and British scientist Francis Crick (1916–2004) announced that they had discovered the double-helix structure of DNA. What the pair had found was more than a bunch of genetic code. They had identified the instructions for making a human being.

Watson and Crick's finding had a huge impact the future of genetic research. It helped scientists understand the genetic cause of diseases, create tests to identify those diseases early, and find new treatments.

Scientists knew that the bases in DNA strands could unzip so that the double helix could copy itself and pass along its genetic information. Later in the century, scientists learned how to copy DNA strands themselves. Once they could copy DNA, they began to insert DNA from one animal into another to introduce new traits. Scientists use this technique, called recombinant DNA technology, to study genes and their function. Once researchers had a handle on how genes worked, the next step was to identify all the thousands of genes contained in every human being.

The Human Genome Project

It takes a lot of instructions to make and operate a human being. Thousands of genes made up of some three billion DNA base pairs form this entire set of instructions, called the human genome. Scientists knew that if they were to understand exactly how genes affect disease, they'd need some sort of road map to the human genome.

A scientist working on the Human Genome Project at the Whitehead
Institute in Cambridge, Massachusetts, uses a sequencing machine to
help decipher the genetic code.

The job of mapping the human genome went to scientists from the National Institutes of Health (NIH) and the U.S. Department of Energy (DOE), and it was performed at several major medical centers throughout the United States. Other scientists from the United Kingdom, France, Germany, Japan, and China helped, too. It was a thirteen-year effort, launched in 1990, called the Human Genome Project.

In April 2003, almost exactly fifty years after Watson and Crick announced the discovery of the DNA double helix, scientists had finished the Human Genome Project. They had learned that humans have some thirty thousand genes—not the one-hundred thousand genes that they had expected to find.

Understanding the genetic code has helped researchers understand the way in which genes work and how they cause disease. Now that scientists have all of the puzzle pieces, the next step is to put them together. They need to understand which parts of the genetic sequence match up with which cell functions to find out exactly how diseases occur and how to stop them from happening.

After researching spina bifida and genetics for more than a century, scientists have figured out that the disease stems from two main triggers: gene changes and environmental factors. What this probably means is that certain families carry altered genes that make them more likely to have spina bifida, but then something must also occur to actually cause the disease.

Genetic Culprits

Investigators have identified a few possible spina bifida suspects in the genetic lineup. One of the most likely groups includes the genes MTHFR, MTR, MTRR, and MTHFD1. These

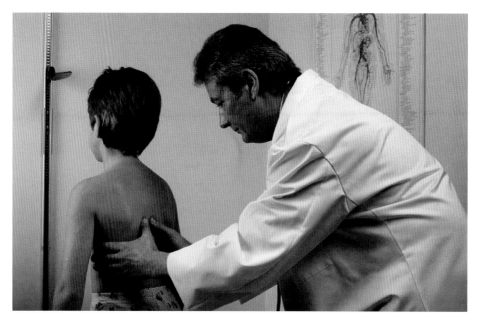

A doctor examines the spine of a young boy. Spinal examination is one method of detecting spina bifida.

genes affect how the body uses folic acid, the nutrient that is needed for the neural tube to form correctly in the fetus.

Scientists think there might be other genes involved as well. Mothers with obesity or diabetes might be more likely to have children affected with spina bifida, for example. Other genes might affect the way the neural tube closes in the fetus.

Because of these genes, spina bifida tends to run in families. Having a parent, brother or sister, grandparent, or cousin with the disease increases a person's risk of also having spina bifida. Parents who have already had one or more children with spina bifida are much more likely to have another baby (or babies) born with the condition.

These are important findings, but the hunt for genes involved in spina bifida is far from over. Scientists are not only searching for new genes that might play a role, but are also trying to figure out how exactly genes and environmental factors work together to cause spina bifida. At present, it's still much of a mystery.

Environmental Factors

Genes are hard to change. Some of the other factors that lead to spina bifida are preventable, though.

Probably the easiest way to prevent spina bifida is for women to take folic acid every day, especially while they are trying to conceive and once they are pregnant. To make sure they're getting enough, women should take a supplement containing at least 400 micrograms (mcg) of folic acid each day. This amount of folic acid is also contained in prenatal multivitamins. Women who are at risk for spina bifida because they have the disease, or they've already had a child with spina bifida, should take 4,000 mcg (4 mg) of folic acid for at least one month before getting pregnant and during their first trimester of pregnancy. According to the Centers for Disease Control and Prevention, taking folic acid daily can reduce the risk of neural tube defects by up to 70 percent. The rates of spina bifida have already dropped significantly since the late 1990s when the government started requiring companies to add folic acid to grain products.

Another big risk for spina bifida is diabetes in the mother. In one form of diabetes, the body doesn't produce insulin. In the other form of diabetes, the body doesn't use insulin properly or is resistant to insulin. Insulin is a hormone that helps the cells use the sugar from food. Without enough insulin, the level of sugar in the blood rises. Diabetes can lead to serious problems, including heart disease, kidney problems, nerve problems, and

People who have diabetes must check their blood glucose (sugar) levels regularly. One way to test blood sugar levels is by using the finger-stick method, which involves a lancet and blood glucose meter.

blindness. A woman with diabetes is more likely to have a baby with spina bifida if she doesn't control her blood sugar levels with medicine and diet.

Obesity is a condition that is often associated with the insulin-resistant form of diabetes, and it is also a risk for spina bifida. By definition, a person who is obese has a body mass index (BMI—a measure of weight in relation to height) greater than 30. Being obese puts you at risk for diabetes, heart disease, joint problems, and many other dangerous health conditions. The higher a woman's BMI, the greater her odds of giving birth to a baby who has spina bifida.

Other risks for giving birth to a baby with spina bifida include the following:

Race. Spina bifida is more common in Caucasians and Hispanics than in African Americans and Asians.

Medications. Mothers who take certain types of medicines used to control seizures, such as valproic acid (Depakote or Depakene) and carbamezapine (Tegretol), are more likely to have a baby with spina bifida. Researchers think these drugs might interfere with the body's use of folic acid.

High temperatures. Running a prolonged high fever during early pregnancy has been connected to spina bifida. Doctors aren't sure whether the illness that causes the fever, or the fever itself, affects spina bifida risk. However, sitting in a hot tub or sauna also seems to increase the risk for spina bifida, so it might be the heat itself.

Agent Orange. This chemical was used to strip the leaves from trees during the Vietnam War so that the U.S. military could see the enemy. Since the war, exposure to Agent Orange in the father has been linked to a higher rate of cancers and birth defects, including spina bifida.

What Spina Bifida Does to the Body

Spina bifida isn't always obvious. In fact, people who have the mildest form, spina bifida occulta, might not even know it except for a hairy, swollen, or discolored patch of skin on their back. Later in life, the damage to their spine can worsen, causing problems such as:

- Loss of feeling (numbness) in the back or legs
- Pain in the back or legs
- Abnormal shape to the legs, feet, or back
- Problems urinating or having bowel movements (because these functions are controlled by nerves in the spine)

Sergeant Stephen Miller of the U.S. Army is shown here in 1994 holding up a picture of his wife, Bianca, and son, Cedrick. Sgt. Miller believes that his exposure to chemicals and radiation during his military service caused his son to develop spina bifida and other birth defects.

People with myelomeningocele often have more serious symptoms, such as unusually shaped bones, paralysis, and trouble controlling their bladder and bowels. Other problems with this more severe form of spina bifida include the following:

Hydrocephalus. In people with myelomeningocele, the brain sits lower than normal and presses down on the spinal cord, blocking the flow of the fluid that protects the brain and spinal cord. When the fluid backs up, pressure builds inside the head. Without treatment to drain the fluid, hydrocephalus can cause mental retardation, nerve problems, seizures, or blindness.

Arnold-Chiari malformation (also called Chiari II malformation). This problem, named for the doctors who described it, is also caused by the abnormal position of the lower part of the brain (cerebellum). It can lead to problems with breathing and swallowing, as well as upper body weakness. Surgery can relieve pressure in the brain.

Tethered spinal cord. Most children with myelomeningocele and some with the other forms of spina bifida have this problem. A piece of tissue holds down the spinal cord so it can't move up and down as it should. A tethered spinal cord can cause leg weakness, curvature of the spine (scoliosis), pain in the back or legs, and bladder problems. Doctors can perform surgery to free the spinal cord from the tissue that holds it.

Latex allergy. Nearly three-quarters of people who have myelomeningocele are allergic to natural rubber (latex), according to the Spina Bifida Association. Doctors often wear latex gloves when performing surgery and other procedures. Children with spina bifida are often exposed to latex many times during their treatments. Over time, they can become sensitive to latex. A latex allergy can cause watery eyes, rash, hives, or trouble breathing (wheezing). Someone who is highly allergic can even die when exposed to latex. Children with spina bifida need to avoid balloons, pacifiers, gloves, and any other products made with latex.

Learning problems. Children with spina bifida are usually just as intelligent as their peers. Sometimes, though, they have problems remembering things they've learned, paying attention, and picking up new math and reading concepts. Some children with spina bifida need extra help in school.

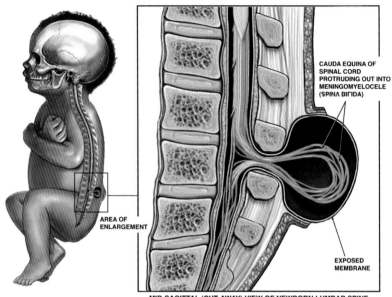

CAUDA EQUINA OF
SPINAL CORD
PROTRUDING OUT INTO
MENINGOMYELOCELE
(SPINA BIFIDA)

AREA OF
ENLARGEMENT

EXPOSED
MEMBRANE

MID-SAGITTAL (CUT-AWAY) VIEW OF NEWBORN LUMBAR SPINE

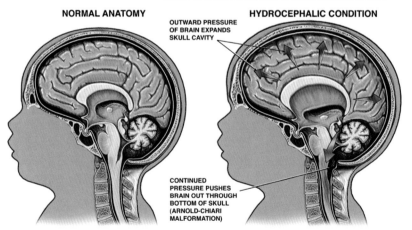

NORMAL ANATOMY

HYDROCEPHALIC CONDITION

OUTWARD PRESSURE
OF BRAIN EXPANDS
SKULL CAVITY

CONTINUED
PRESSURE PUSHES
BRAIN OUT THROUGH
BOTTOM OF SKULL
(ARNOLD-CHIARI
MALFORMATION)

The top illustration shows the exposed spinal cord sticking out through the back in a child with myelomeningocele. The bottom illustration shows the pressure in the brain from hydrocephalus and the abnormal position of the brain in Arnold-Chiari malformation, two complications of spina bifida.

JEFFREY'S STORY

Some children who have spina bifida develop a condition called hydrocephalus. Many of them need to have surgery to implant a shunt so that too much pressure doesn't build up in the brain. Most of the time shunts work very well. Sometimes, though, problems can occur during surgery or with the shunt itself.

That's what happened to Jeffrey, the son of CNN anchor Judy Woodruff. He was born with spina bifida. Shortly after birth, he had surgery to close his spine, and he had surgery again a few months later to implant a shunt to treat his hydrocephalus.

Despite his condition, Jeffrey was very much like any other child his age. He could walk, swim, ski, and ride a bicycle. Then when Jeffrey was sixteen, doctors found a problem with his shunt and he had to have another surgery to correct it. During the surgery, there were complications. Afterward, Jeffrey was no longer able to walk. He was also unable to move the right side of his body, talk clearly, or see well.

Today, Jeffrey is in his twenties. Although he must use a wheelchair to get around, he is still able to smile and laugh, just as he did before his surgery. His mother has been helping to get the word out about spina bifida. She hopes that other women will take folic acid while they are pregnant to help prevent this condition in their own babies.

CNN anchor Judy Woodruff poses at home with her son, Jeffrey, who has spina bifida.

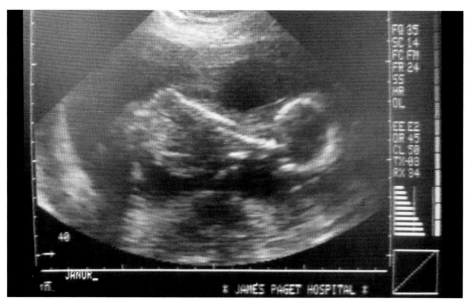

An ultrasound, which uses sound waves to create a two-dimensional picture of the fetus inside its mother, is one of the techniques doctors employ to help them diagnose spina bifida before a baby is born.

Spotting Spina Bifida Early

Thanks to better test methods, doctors can find out whether a baby has spina bifida before he or she is even born. At about four or five months into a woman's pregnancy, her doctor will recommend taking a sample of her blood. The blood is tested for a protein called alpha-fetoprotein (AFP), which is made by the fetus. High AFP levels can (but don't always) mean that the baby has spina bifida or another developmental defect.

Sometimes, the test will also look for other substances produced by the fetus. These substances can show the presence of not only neural tube defects such as spina bifida, but also Down syndrome and other chromosome problems. This test is

THE SPINA BIFIDA ASSOCIATION

While scientists search for ways to treat or prevent spina bifida, the Spina Bifida Association (SBA) is helping children live with the effects of the disease today. The organization offers a number of programs and services, including:

◀ Internet discussion boards for parents and children
◀ A scholarship fund for young people with spina bifida
◀ Mentors who take children on field trips and teach them how to become more independent
◀ Summer camps so that children with spina bifida have a place where they don't have to feel different from others

To contact the Spina Bifida Association, see the For More Information section at the end of this book.

called the triple screen test (when it tests for three substances) or the quad screen test (when it tests for four substances).

Positive test results might lead the doctor to recommend an ultrasound. An ultrasound uses high-energy sound waves to create a picture of the baby on a small monitor. This test can show the doctor any problems in the baby's spine that might be signs of spina bifida. Some parents might want to know during pregnancy if their baby may have a neural tube defect, while other parents might not want to know.

The mother might also have an amniocentesis. The doctor inserts a needle into her belly and pulls out a small sample of fluid (called amniotic fluid) from around the fetus. The doctor can check this fluid for high AFP levels. (Many women usually decide to have multiple ultrasounds during their pregnancies because that imaging technique is widely available. They prefer not to have the invasive procedure of amniocentesis, where a needle is inserted into the body.)

JEAN DRISCOLL

Jean Driscoll is an Olympic athlete, a marathon winner, and a motivational speaker. She's achieved things that most people only dream about doing. What makes Driscoll even more amazing is that she's completed all of these goals while confined to a wheelchair with spina bifida.

Driscoll was born on November 18, 1966, in Milwaukee, Wisconsin. Although she was born with spina bifida, she never let her physical disability stop her from accomplishing what she wanted to do. As a wheelchair racer, she was the only athlete in

history to win the Boston Marathon eight times. She also won two Olympic silver medals and twelve Paralympic medals. In 2000, *Sports Illustrated for Women* named Driscoll one of the Top 100 Female Athletes of the Twentieth Century. Today, Driscoll helps other people with disabilities learn how to follow their dreams.

Jean Driscoll crosses the finish line to win the women's division of the 1996 Boston Marathon.

Treatments

Sadly, there is no known cure for spina bifida at this time. Prevention is very important. However, treatments can greatly improve the quality of life for people who have the condition.

Because it is so mild, spina bifida occulta doesn't usually need any treatment. Meningocele can be fixed with surgery, and most babies who have the condition can learn to walk after having treatment.

Fixing myelomeningocele is more complicated. Babies who are born with this type of spina bifida must have surgery within a few days of birth. The surgeon will put the nerves and spinal cord back into the baby's spinal canal, close the opening in the back, and cover it with skin. If the baby also has hydrocephalus, the doctor will place a tube called a shunt inside the baby's brain to drain fluid. The child will likely have to have a shunt for his or her entire life.

Although surgery can prevent infection and stop the spinal cord from being damaged further, it can't fix the injury that has already been done to the spine. The child might need to use braces or crutches to walk. A physical therapist can help children with this condition learn how to walk correctly. Some children with severe myelomeningoceles can't walk at all, though, and will need to use a wheelchair.

Hope for People with Spina Bifida

With the right treatment, people who have spina bifida can live very full and productive lives. Thanks to new and improved surgeries, about 90 percent of babies born with spina bifida live into adulthood, according to the Spina Bifida Association. About 80 percent have normal IQ scores, and about 75 percent take part in sports and other activities.

The Search for a Cure

Researchers have gone on the hunt for spina bifida genes. They've already found a few genes that they think might lead to the disease, but they believe more exist. Once they are found, these genes can provide important clues to how the disease occurs. Knowing which genes are involved might one day lead to better treatments—or even cures—for spina bifida.

The Search for the Gene in Mice

In 1999, scientists at Royal Melbourne Hospital in Australia discovered something very interesting in fruit flies. They found a mutation, or change, to a gene that stopped the fly's back

Scientists study mice to learn about the genes that cause spina bifida in humans. In this picture, the mouse skeleton on the left has spina bifida—the vertebrae in the middle section of its spinal column are open.

from closing properly. Because babies born with spina bifida have the same problem, the researchers thought that there might be a similar genetic flaw in humans.

In 2003, the researchers announced a major breakthrough: they had found the gene that causes spina bifida in mice. The normal gene causes a mouse's spinal cord to close properly. When they removed the suspected gene from mice (called "knockout mice") that were still in the embryo stage, those mice were born with spina bifida. This was the first time that a spina bifida gene had been discovered. The researchers believe the faulty gene in mice is the same gene found in humans with spina bifida.

The researchers say this gene might be the reason why some people get spina bifida, even when their mothers took folic acid before and during pregnancy. They believe the gene makes people resistant to the effects of folic acid.

Another breakthrough in the search for spina bifida genes came in 2005. In that year, scientists at the Texas Institute for Genomic Medicine said they had found defects in a gene called FKBP8, which they think is involved in spina bifida. Scientists used knockout mice with an altered FKBP8 gene to show the effects of spina bifida. All of the mice that had a defective form of this gene developed the disease. The researchers said their finding might one day prevent spina bifida if this defective gene can be fixed, and it could also improve the lives of people who already have the disease.

KNOCKOUT MICE

Studying mice can teach scientists a lot about human disease. That's because mice and humans, although very different on the outside, share many of the same genes.

To study genes in mice, scientists remove, or "knock out," some of the genes in a mouse embryo and replace them with artificial pieces of DNA. Depending on the gene involved, this change affects something about the mouse: its appearance, behavior, or health. By studying the changes that occur, scientists can learn the function of the genes. (This technology is also called gene targeting.)

Using knockout mice has helped scientists understand many diseases, such as cancer, diabetes, immune problems, and heart disease. The technique is also helping them study spina bifida.

Once scientists had found spina bifida genes in mice, the next step was to look for the genes in human DNA.

Human Spina Bifida Genes

In 2007, scientists for the first time discovered spina bifida genes in humans. Researchers at McGill University in Montreal, Quebec, Canada, found three mutations in a gene called VANGL1 that they said increase the risk for spina bifida. Scientists have found similar mutations in this gene in some French and Italian children with spina bifida.

Although this finding may not yet lead to a cure for the disease, it could help doctors diagnose spina bifida. Also, it might be used to determine which parents are most likely to have a baby with spina bifida. This knowledge could one day help prevent future cases of the disease.

Scientists believe that not one, but many genes come together to cause spina bifida. Now they are looking for more of those genes. The Duke Center for Human Genetics in North Carolina has launched a project that includes more than two thousand families that have at least one member with a neural tube defect. The researchers are taking DNA samples from members of those families and are scanning them for genes that cause or might lead to neural tube defects.

Another research effort, the Spina Bifida Research Resource (SBRR), is looking at families with neural tube defects. Researchers on this project are using the DNA in blood and saliva samples from people with spina bifida, as well as from their parents and grandparents. In those samples, the researchers will look for genes that affect how the body uses folic acid from foods and vitamins. They will also look for the genes that hold the instructions that the spinal cord needs

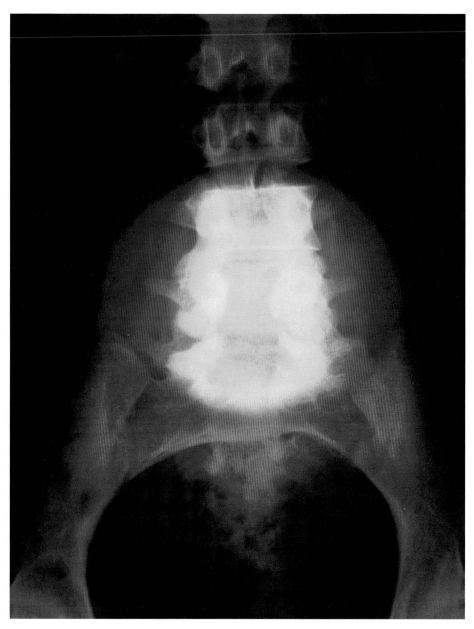

This color X-ray of a spina bifida patient's vertebrae shows a myelomeningocele *(in blue)* in the lower lumbar vertebrae.

Ten Great Questions to Ask a Doctor

1. How does somebody get spina bifida?

2. How common is spina bifida?

3. How is the condition treated?

4. Is there a cure for spina bifida?

5. Are children who have spina bifida able to walk?

6. What is the outlook for children with spina bifida?

7. Is there a risk for spina bifida in my family?

8. Is it possible to reduce the risk of getting spina bifida?

9. What is folic acid and how can I get it?

10. How much folic acid do I need?

to develop properly. This study is set to finish in 2011, and it should tell scientists much more about the genetic causes of spina bifida.

The Famous Faces of Spina Bifida

These celebrities have all proved that it is possible to achieve great success while living with spina bifida:

Robert Hensel—In 2000, Hensel was chosen as one of the best poets of the twentieth century. He also holds the world's record for the longest nonstop wheelie. He traveled more than 6.178 miles (9.943 kilometers) tipped back on the wheels of his wheelchair to promote awareness of wheelchair accessibility.

Frida Kahlo—This highly respected Mexican artist was believed to have had constant leg and back pain due to spina bifida. She often painted images of sick bodies, probably to reflect her own condition.

Rene Kirby—In the movie *Shallow Hal* with Jack Black and Gwyneth Paltrow, Kirby played a character named Walt, who has spina bifida. Kirby didn't have to study too hard for the part because he has the condition in real life. This successful actor has also appeared in *Stuck on You* with Matt Damon and Greg Kinnear, and in the HBO series *Carnivale*.

Hank Williams Sr.—Born in Alabama in 1923 with spina bifida occulta, Williams went on to become one of the most famous performers in the history of country music.

The Latest Spina Bifida Treatments

For many decades now, doctors have been performing surgery on newborns with spina bifida. This surgery closes the baby's back to prevent infection, which used to kill almost every baby who was born with the disease.

In the 1990s, doctors tried something new: they started performing the surgery while the baby was still in the mother's womb. The hope is that fixing the problem early might prevent some of the problems, such as paralysis, that normally occur in children with spina bifida.

During the surgery, the doctor gives anesthesia to both the mother and fetus so that they sleep and don't feel any pain.

A modern art exhibit in Mexico City displays some of the paintings of Mexican artist Frida Kahlo (1907–1954), who was supposedly born with spina bifida.

Then the surgeon makes a cut in the mother's uterus and lifts out the baby. The doctor fixes the spine defect and covers up the baby's back. Then, the baby is placed back inside the uterus, which is closed up.

The big question is whether this surgery really helps. Doctors want to be sure that it works because performing surgery while the baby is still in the womb is risky and can cause the baby to be delivered too early (prematurely). Premature birth can cause many health risks in the baby.

To learn the best time to perform the surgery, a number of researchers are involved in a study called the Management of Myelomeningocele (MOMS). The study at three centers—

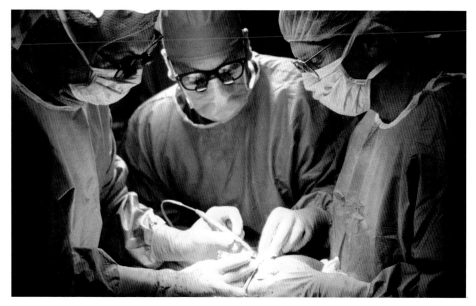

Doctors at Vanderbilt University Medical Center in Nashville, Tennessee, perform surgery on a fetus with spina bifida. Vanderbilt's physicians have pioneered methods for treating spina bifida in the womb.

the University of California, San Francisco; the Children's Hospital of Philadelphia; and Vanderbilt University Medical Center in Nashville—compares surgery before birth to surgery after birth in two hundred babies with the most severe kind of spina bifida.

So far, the initial results have been mixed. Surgery before birth seems to prevent some babies from later needing shunts in their brain due to hydrocephalus. Other babies have not shown any improvement. Fetal surgery doesn't seem to help children walk any better, though. Doctors will have to wait for the final results to know more about the benefits of early surgery.

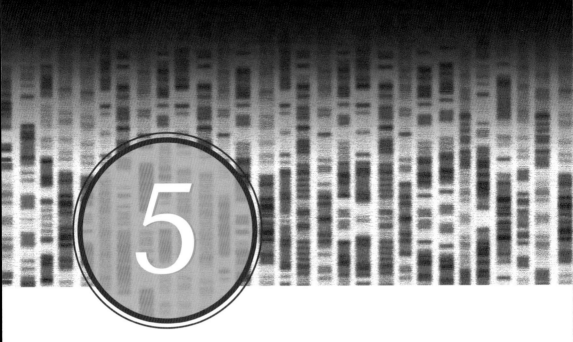

Scientists are busy looking for more clues into the causes of spina bifida. They've already found a few genetic changes in mice and some in humans that they believe can cause the disease. The next step is to find the rest of the missing genetic puzzle pieces.

Once they've found all of the spina bifida genes, scientists might be able to develop better genetic tests so that people will know whether they carry genes for the disease before they have children. Understanding how spina bifida genes work—for example, how genes help the spinal cord to close in the fetus— could lead to better ways of treating, or even preventing, the disease.

Scientists are also studying gene therapy, which uses a virus or other vessel to carry the

A medical researcher injects DNA into a cell to change its genetic material. Research like this is helping scientists develop new tests and treatments for spina bifida.

correct gene into cells to replace ones that are defective. Right now, gene therapy isn't being used for spina bifida, but that might change in the future. One day, it might even be possible to stop the disease that today continues to cripple children in the womb.

Other research is looking at folic acid. It's already known to reduce the risk of spina bifida by 50 percent to 70 percent. Now researchers want to find out why it works and learn ways to make it even more effective.

In other areas of research, scientists are looking at new and different types of tests that can be done during pregnancy to find out if a fetus has spina bifida. Finally, they're trying to improve the lives of children who already have the disease.

GENETIC TESTING

Scientists aren't magicians, but sometimes they can predict the future. Genes are helping them learn which people are likely to get a disease long before the first symptom appears.

With genetic testing, doctors take a sample, usually of the blood, and look at the DNA in the cells. Then they search for the gene that causes a particular disease. A positive test means that you have the gene, but it doesn't always mean that you will definitely develop the disease. Some diseases, like spina bifida, are caused by both genes and environmental factors.

Right now, genetic tests can look for hundreds of different diseases. Scientists are trying to develop even more tests. Testing can be done in people of any age, even before a baby is born.

The Promise—and Perils— of Genetic Research

Say that scientists are able to find all of the genes that cause spina bifida. What happens then? Some people are worried about the possible risks of knowing too much about the genes that cause disease.

If people can change genes in order to prevent disease, couldn't they also change the genes responsible for eye color, height, or intelligence? Some people fear that this would lead to "designer babies," who are created to be as close to perfect as possible. Another worry is that the government or insurance companies might get their hands on genetic test results. Could

Matthew Alexander, who has spina bifida, leads the cheerleading squad of Ardmore Middle School in Oklahoma in a cheer in 2001. Scientists are trying to develop new treatments for spina bifida to help people like Alexander who are living with the disease.

an insurance company refuse to cover someone just because he or she has a family history of disease? Might the government keep a close watch on someone who carries the genes for mental illness?

All of these possibilities raise important ethical issues about genetic testing. Right now, though, scientists are focusing on the many possible benefits that genes can provide to people at risk for spina bifida and for many other genetic diseases.

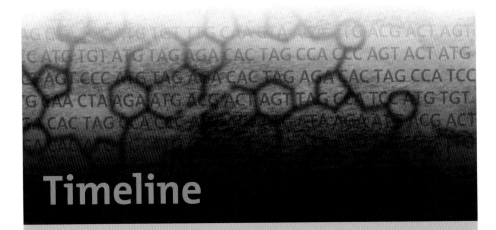

Timeline

10000–8500 BCE
Skeletons with possible spina bifida dating back from this time period are found in Taforalt, Morocco.

1652
Dutch anatomist Nicolaas Tulp names spina bifida and gives the first real description of the disease.

1761
Italian doctor Giovanni Battista Morgagni connects hydrocephalus with spina bifida.

1859
Charles Darwin publishes *The Origin of the Species*, which suggests that there is a way to pass altered traits from one generation to another.

1866
Austrian monk Gregor Mendel publishes *Experiments in Plant Hybridisation*, in which he describes how traits are passed down from one generation to another.

1869
Johann Friedrich Miescher discovers "nuclein" (DNA) in white blood cells.

1875
German doctor Rudolf Virchow coins the term "spina bifida occulta."

1891

Hans Chiari describes abnormalities of the brain that are now known as Chiari type II malformations and often occur with myelomeningocele.

1952

The shunt is introduced to drain fluid from the brain in children with hydrocephalus.

1953

James Watson and Francis Crick discover the double-helix structure of DNA.

1965

Richard Smithells and E. D. Hibbard connect spina bifida with a lack of folic acid.

1971

John Lorber develops controversial criteria to determine which children should be treated for spina bifida.

1980s

The maternal serum alpha-fetoprotein (MSAFP) blood test becomes available to screen for neural tube defects.

1993

Duke University scientists begin enrolling patients in their study, "Hereditary Basis of Neural Tube Defects," which looks for the genes involved in spina bifida.

1998

The first fetal surgery for myelomeningocele is done to close the spine while a baby is still in the womb.

The Spina Bifida Research Resource study begins at Texas A&M University. It looks at DNA from patients with spina bifida to find genetic and environmental risk factors for spina bifida. The study is due to be completed in 2011.

2003

The Human Genome Project—an effort to map the entire genetic information in human beings—is finished.

Researchers in Australia find a gene in mice that is linked to spina bifida.

MOMS (Management of Myelomeningocele Study) begins enrollment at three major U.S. medical centers; it should be completed in 2008.

2005

Scientists at the Texas Institute for Genomic Medicine identify FKBP8, another gene thought to be involved in spina bifida, in mice.

2007

Researchers at McGill University in Toronto identify mutations in VANGL1, a human gene thought to be involved in spina bifida.

The incidence of neural tube defects has been reduced by 50 percent to 70 percent since folic acid supplementation began in the late 1990s.

Glossary

Agent Orange A chemical used in the Vietnam War to strip the leaves from trees. Exposure to it has been linked to diseases, such as cancer, and birth defects.

alpha-fetoprotein A substance in the spinal fluid around the fetus. Raised levels of this substance in the mother's blood are linked to the presence of neural tube defects.

amniocentesis A test that pulls a small amount of fluid from around the fetus to test for genetic problems.

Arnold-Chiari malformation (Chiari II malformation) A problem caused by the abnormal position of the brain. It can lead to difficulties with breathing and swallowing.

body mass index (BMI) A measure of weight in relation to height.

chromosomes Structures found in the cell nucleus that contain DNA.

complications Difficult or involved factors or issues that often appear unexpectedly and change existing plans or methods, as in complications during surgery.

deoxyribonucleic acid (DNA) The double-stranded material inside the cell nucleus that carries genetic information.

diabetes A disease in which a person's body either doesn't make insulin (a hormone needed for the cells to use sugar from foods) or doesn't use it properly.

ethical Consistent with the accepted principles of right and wrong governing the conduct of a group.

folic acid A B vitamin needed for the body to function properly and for the fetus to grow. Taking folic acid before and during pregnancy can help prevent spina bifida and other neural tube defects.

genes Segments of DNA that carry the instructions for making proteins.

hydrocephalus A problem that occurs in people with myelomeningocele. Fluid does not drain normally and builds up in the brain.

latex A natural rubber to which some people with spina bifida are allergic.

meningocele The rarest form of spina bifida. The spine is open, and a sac containing the protective coatings of the brain and spine (meninges) comes through.

mutation A change in a gene that can lead to disease.

myelomeningocele The most severe form of spina bifida. The protective coatings of the spine (meninges) and the spinal nerves stick out through a hole in the back.

neural tube A structure in the fetus that grows into the brain and spinal cord.

neural tube defects A group of birth defects, including spina bifida and anencephaly, that occur when the neural tube doesn't develop correctly in the fetus.

spina bifida occulta The mildest form of spina bifida. It occurs when there is a small opening in the vertebrae but no damage to the spinal cord itself.

For More Information

Birth Defect Research for Children, Inc.
800 Celebration Avenue, Suite 225
Celebration, FL 34747
(407) 566-8304
Web site: http://www.birthdefects.org
This nonprofit organization provides information and support services to parents of children with birth defects. It sponsors the National Birth Defects Registry, which helps researchers study the connection between birth defects and exposure to radiation, smoking, chemicals, and other toxins.

Easter Seals
230 West Monroe Street, Suite 1800
Chicago, IL 60606
(800) 221-6827
Web site: http://www.easterseals.com
Easter Seals, known for the red and white lily logo on its "seals" (stamps), funds services, including physical rehabilitation and job training, for people with disabilities.

March of Dimes Birth Defects Foundation
1275 Mamaroneck Avenue
White Plains, NY 10605
(914) 997-4488

Web site: http://www.marchofdimes.com
The March of Dimes was founded in 1921 to help find an end to the polio epidemic that swept the United States. Once a vaccine for polio was developed, the organization turned its attention to helping prevent premature birth and birth defects.

National Center on Birth Defects and Developmental
   Disabilities (NCBDDD)
Centers for Disease Control and Prevention
1600 Clifton Road
Atlanta, GA 30333
(800) CDC-INFO (232-4636)
Web site: http://www.cdc.gov/ncbddd
This arm of the Centers for Disease Control and Prevention focuses on preventing birth defects and helping people who have birth defects live fuller lives.

National Spinal Cord Injury Association (NSCIA)
1 Church Street, #600
Rockville, MD 20850
Toll-free helpline (800) 962-9629
Website: http://www.spinalcord.org
The NSCIA strives to assist people who have spinal injuries and disease attaining the highest level of independence, quality of life, and personal fulfillment possible, and it provides information services and peer support to these individuals.

Spina Bifida Association
4590 MacArthur Boulevard NW
Washington, DC 20007
(202) 944-3285
Web site: http://www.sbaa.org
Since 1973, the Spina Bifida Association has been working to improve the lives of people with spina bifida.

Spina Bifida and Hydrocephalus Canada
#977-167 Lombard Avenue
Winnipeg, MB R3B 0V3
Canada
(800) 565-9488
Web site: http://www.sbhac.ca/beta/index.php
This Canadian organization has been working since the early 1980s to help people with spina bifida and their families.

Web Sites

Due to the changing nature of Internet links, Rosen Publishing has developed an online list of Web sites related to the subject of this book. This site is updated regularly. Please use this link to access the list:

http://www.rosenlinks.com/gddd/spbi

For Further Reading

Appelmann, Larry E. *Living with Spina Bifida: Speaking Out About My Disability.* Victoria, BC, Canada: Trafford Publishing, 2002.

Arons, Marsha. *Teen Miracles. Extraordinary Life-Changing Stories from Today's Teens.* Cincinnati, OH: Adams Media Corporation, 2004.

Dicken, Janny J. *Cody's Story: Living One Day at a Time with Spina Bifida.* Frederick, MD: PublishAmerica, 2005.

Driscoll, Jean, Janet Benge, and Geoff Benge. *Determined to Win: The Overcoming Spirit of Jean Driscoll.* Colorado Springs, CO: Shaw Books, 2001.

Kaufman, Miriam. *Easy for You to Say: Q and As for Teens Living with Chronic Illness or Disabilities.* Revised ed. Buffalo, NY: Firefly Books, 2005.

Lutkenhoff, Marlene, and Sonya G. Oppenheimer, eds. *Spinabilities: A Young Person's Guide to Spina Bifida.* Bethesda, MD: Woodbine House, 1997.

Thornton, Denise. *Physical Disabilities: The Ultimate Teen Guide* (It Happened to Me). Lanham, MD: Scarecrow Press, 2007.

Bibliography

Centers for Disease Control and Prevention. "Use of Dietary
Supplements Containing Folic Acid Among Women of
Childbearing Age—United States, 2005." *Morbidity Mortality
Weekly Report*, Vol. 54, No. 38, September 30, 2005, pp.
955–958.

Dunn, Amanda. "Researchers Unlock Spina Bifida Mystery,
Paving Way for Genetic Test." November 11, 2003. Retrieved
August 6, 2007 (http://www.smh.com.au/articles/2003/11/10/
1068329488424.html).

El Din, Azza Mohamed Sarry, and Rokia Abd El-Shafy El Banna.
"Congenital Anomalies of the Vertebral Column: A Case
Study on Ancient and Modern Egypt." *International Journal
of Osteoarchaeology*, Vol. 16, No. 3, May/June 2006, pp.
200–207.

Kibar, Zoha, Elena Torban, Jonathan R. McDearmid, Annie
Reynolds, Joanne Berghout, Melissa Mathieu, Irena Kirillova,
Patrizia De Marco, Elisa Merello, Julie M. Hayes, John B.
Wallingford, Pierre Drapeau, Valeria Capra, and Philippe
Gros. "Mutations in VANGL1 Associated with Neural-Tube
Defects." *New England Journal of Medicine*, Vol. 356,
No. 14, April 5, 2007, pp. 1,432–1,437.

March of Dimes. "Spina Bifida." April 2006. Retrieved August 3,
2007 (http://www.marchofdimes.com/pnhec/4439_1224.asp).

Mitchell, Laura E., N. Scott Adzick, Jeanne Melchionne, and Patrick S. Pasquariello. "Spina Bifida." *Lancet*, Vol. 364, No. 9448, November 20–26, 2004, pp. 1,885–1,895.

National Center for Health Statistics, Centers for Disease Control and Prevention. "Trends in Spina Bifida and Anencephalus in the United States, 1991–2004." Retrieved August 3, 2007 (http://www.cdc.gov/nchs/products/pubs/pubd/hestats/spine_anen.htm).

Neville-Jan, Ann. "The Problem with Prevention: The Case of Spina Bifida." *American Journal of Occupational Therapy*, Vol. 59, No. 5, September/October 2005, pp. 527–539.

Sandler, Adrian, MD. *Living with Spina Bifida: A Guide for Families and Professionals.* Chapel Hill, NC: The University of North Carolina Press, 1997.

Spina Bifida Association. "Spotlight on Spina Bifida." Retrieved August 6, 2007 (http://www.sbaa.org/site/c.liKWL7PLLrF/b.2725873/k.6980/Spotlight_On_SpinaBifida.htm).

Ting, Stephen B., Tomasz Wilanowski, Alana Auden, Mark Hall, Anne K. Voss, Tim Thomas, Vishwas Parekh, John M. Cunningham, and Stephen M. Jane. "Inositol- and Folate-Resistant Neural Tube Defects in Mice Lacking the Epithelial-Specific Factor Grhl-3." *Nature Medicine*, Vol. 9, published online November 9, 2003, pp. 1,513–1,519.

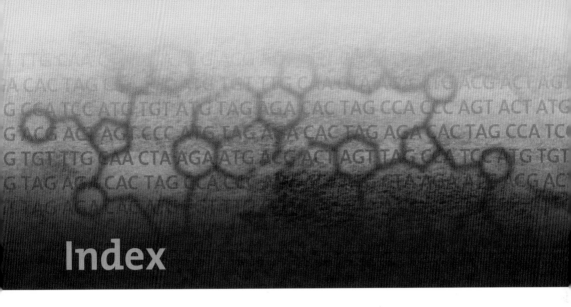

Index

A

adenine, 16
Agent Orange, 28
alpha-fetoprotein, 15, 33, 34
amniocentesis, 34, 35
anencephaly, 5
Aristotle, 10

B

body mass index, 27
Brock, D. J., 14–15

C

carbamezapine, 28
Chiari, Hans, 10
Chiari type II malformations
    (Arnold-Chiari malformations),
    11, 30
chromosomes, 16, 17
Crick, Francis, 21, 23
cytosine, 16

D

Darwin, Charles, 18–19
"designer babies," 48

diabetes, 25, 26–27, 39
DNA, explanation of, 16, 19, 21
Down syndrome, 18, 33
Driscoll, Jean, 35
Duke Center for Human Genetics, 40

E

encephalocele, 5

F

fetal surgery, 43–45
FKBP8 gene, 39
folic acid, 8, 14, 20, 25, 26, 28, 32,
    39, 40, 47

G

genes, explanation of, 16–17, 21–23
gene targeting, 39
gene therapy, 46–47
genetic mutations, 18
genetic testing, 48
guanine, 16

H

Hensel, Robert, 42–43
Hibbard, E. D., 14

hidden spina bifida, 6
high temperatures, spina bifida
     and, 28
Hippocrates, 10
Human Genome Project, 21–23
Huntington's disease, 18
hydrocephalus, 7, 10, 12, 13, 29,
     32, 36, 45

I

insulin, 26

K

Kahlo, Frida, 43
Kirby, Rene, 43

L

latex allergy, 30
learning problems, 30
Lorber, John, 13

M

Management of
     Myelomeningocele, 44
March of Dimes, 14
maternal alpha-fetoprotein test, 15
medications, spina bifida and, 28
Mendel, Gregor, 17–18, 19
meningocele, 6–7, 36
Miescher, Johann Friedrich, 19
Morgagni, Giovanni Battista, 10
MTHFD1 gene, 24–25
MTHFR gene, 24–25
MTR gene, 24–25
MTRR gene, 24–25
myelomeningocele, 6, 7, 29,
     30, 36

N

National Institutes of Health, 23
natural selection, 19
neural tube/neural tube defects, 4,
     5, 8, 14, 15, 25, 26, 33, 34, 40

O

obesity, 25, 27
Observationes Medicae, 10
open spina bifida, 7
Origin of Species, The, 18–19

Q

quad screen test, 15, 34

R

race, spina bifida and, 27–28
recombinant DNA technology, 21

S

shunts, 12, 13, 32, 36, 45
Smithells, Richard, 14
spina bifida
     early/prenatal detection of, 14–15,
          33–35
     environmental factors for, 8,
          26–28
     explanation of, 4
     famous people with, 42–43
     genetic factors of, 8, 24–26,
          37–42
     history of, 9–15
     myths and facts about, 20
     statistics on, 4, 5, 6, 36
     treatments for, 36, 43–45
     types of, 6–7
     what it does to the body, 28–30

Spina Bifida Association, 6, 30,
    34, 36
spina bifida occulta, 6, 10, 28, 36
Spina Bifida Research Resource, 40
surgery, 5, 7, 12–13, 30, 32, 36, 43–45
Sutcliffe, R. G., 14–15

T

tethered spinal cord, 30
thymine, 16
triple screen test, 15, 34
Tulp, Nicolaas, 10

U

ultrasounds, 34
U.S. Department of Energy, 23

V

valproic acid, 28
VANGL1 gene, 40
Virchow, Rudolf, 10

W

Watson, James, 21, 23
Williams, Hank, Sr., 43

About the Author

Stephanie Watson is a writer and editor based in Atlanta, Georgia. She has written or contributed to more than a dozen health and science books, including *Endometriosis, Encyclopedia of the Human Body: The Endocrine System, The Mechanisms of Genetics: An Anthology of Current Thought*, and *Science and Its Times*. Watson's work has also been featured on several health and wellness Web sites, including Rosen's Teen Health & Wellness database.

Photo Credits